AF392528

Small Talk

Small Talk
By Blace Alcock

Dedicated to Launchpad and its' incredible
current and former staff:

> Jorja-Rae Lardy
> Chris Hoekstra
> Nicholas Manglal-lan
> Josh
> Daniel Casadio
> Lauren Schierz

If it wasn't for your support, this book
likely wouldn't have been made.

Introduction

In the blank infinity stretched across, there are words. Long, winding strings of them forming cohesion which plays with the senses. They enliven the mind and the body, they transform the mundane, and they make you relate these feelings to what you read forever. That's my aim as a poet, to create experiences and share what I find most beautiful in the world; tragic or otherwise. But every introduction must begin with small talk before we can wax poetic about existence. With that being said, let me welcome you and I hope you stay till the end.

Midnight Voyage

Summerset plains melted into the distant horizon
Waves flailed against our ship
Salt carrassed you, our figurehead,
While we drifted through the blue

You found this vacation strenuous,
Subsuming leisure in placid tedium
You forgoed an interim, and
I abandoned my relaxation, my
Books and soft chair, for you
Who I sat by and wrote about

"I'm Hopeless". You said,
But I wrote, trying to embrace your depths
"I do this all the time, why bother taking me anywhere?"
I didn't answer

Silence's pendulum swung between us when you said
"...I hate it here"
I read what I had written.

We are on a midnight voyage
Free of salt from cities,
Brimming with sirens and desperate screams.
While you Mourned yourself, I
Was entrenched in you,
In love, as if meeting you for the first time

Ease into our dreams
Lounge for a haft a moment, so
The figurehead can admit she matters
She's Worth Something
On this midnight Voyage

She's A Mirror

(Dinner time)

And we sat there eating and laughing,
She invited me to guess her soul's inner clockwork.
Chinese food I believe we ate

Her soul was a crystalized tarn
Hardened by pressure, for age had seized *something*,
But she steered into cloudy heights; joyful luminaries.
Bewildered, she said "you're something else"

I'm louisiana grass beds entangled within the rotted beliefs
I'm chapel steeples grasping for heaven
Jerusalem's bells are my lullabies

But I saw my reflection in her soul,
Her bliss washed over me.
Panicked, I turned when she smiled and took my hand
"You're something else", she reassured.

Geometrical

Volumes amass in cubicles of nothing,

Where they jitter amid infinite symmetry.

Division breeds nature

An ever-shifting sphere sows new forms
Atlas bears with reserved contempt.
Universal Anatomy sculpts that podium,

Yet the moon, who's faces wail geometric purity,
Refrains to edges while our contours deepen.
The Sun revolves as time bleeds,
Not a second too late

Rene Rochester

Grievous, O Rochester, locked in that Palace of twilight desire.
A sophisticated cage populated with every freedom,
Yet its boredom which choked the painter.
The gorgeous hands of artificial love torturing the painter.
The tenuous bramble reality clawing at his sanity;
O Rochester, suicide will free you of yourself.

Fragmented Rites of Godhood

Sun-locked on a divine dias
Where the throne Merkabah chanted to heavens and earth.
It bellowed to the Mem-Aleph
Suspended on the universes' branches.
Oh, holy, mighty, transcendental glory,
I beg thee to suffer one utterance of my pleas.

Leper Festivities

Opaque masks shudder beneath hacking fits
The ill bay tirelessly, for
Their disease immerses every mirror.

While the party's flesh cracks,
Dance floors sluggishly arouse,
And pox mottled hands quiver in marble passages.
Kings and queens descend into their ancient tapestries
Yet, few waltz anymore, all their feet are clubbed;
They stand at corners watching those who can

Do plagues engage in intimate warfare?
Their infantries are lovers who mingle
And recede, reconciling from trenches;
Their excitement reassures
But their hands eclipse the future

The Audience

Remembered this show, meeting

Its' curtains with rabid bays.
An Addict stumbled on stage
Rags hung off his shoulders.
When he jammed a needle into his arm, a
Stagelight beamed on his sallow face, and
The first act began
"I... I... I am an... Actor
Shakespearean at heart! Basking
In near infinity, my...
Life enclosed by it"
He swilled from a flask
While he wiped his mouth,
The addict mocked the audience
And they loved it, told by a man of higher standing
Everything wrong with them.
Five acts after were the same,
Mocking, jeering, empathetic as any actor
Yet, when they went to retrieve him,
At the end, he was lying there
On the corner of the stage, dead
And the audience reveled.

Fallen Angel

HOLY, HOLY, HOLY

Is the LORD of hosts set in his gilded throne
Holy art thou moulded by his hands and
Holy art thou who still admires The Father.

He cratered from heaven on wings of pride
And slumped at a cliff, watching his siblings chant their worship
Their song pierced the firmament's edge, where Satan festered
He quivered, sneering, he tossed an arm over his face
Alas, a single tear squirmed to a lips' corner
While he scoffed his wings wilted, so
He abandoned them and descended into hell

Holy is the heart of Satan
He who loves his LORD unconditionally,
Even as he sat amongst banshee souls crying for repentence
Holy is he who loathes
How he will never stop loving the LORD

Inspiration
(Nothing is Ever Original)

She was a brown haired delight

Fairer than moon's glow, who's shafts split clouds–
Who's hand brushed her hair
As a carpenter entered with designs tucked under an arm

We hope to restore it all,
Are there any additions you wish?
Make me original, she said

They unfastened it all, left her barren
Devoid of the waves that spilled over her shoulders.
Am I still beautiful? She Pondered
She was too much of a good thing

But love is blind, deaf, ravaged, torn
Yet, everything else captivated:
Her eyes, lips like glossed pearls, and a heart of gold
Which seized its' treasured horde effortlessly

The carpenters marched forth groping their hammers
And chisels, where they incised the hairs.
While they finished, she remarked–
Like whispers through trees–
Next time we'll try for something original;
Onyx embedded with glittering stars

Or perhaps a bob cut blacker than any night sky
Something original maybe

Passionfruit

Beckon not shells from seas,

Who's shattered faces scream in awe–
But regard yourself.
Passionfruit sandals trampling Eden soil
Disappearing into mesh field
And plastic forests, where
The Putto sings its' gospels–
For none chime bells like angelic prophets,
Who brandish swords aflame as they melt into heaven.
And The Father proclaims saintly reminders,
And The Christ proclaims:
Agony forever

A Handful of Change

She's a bursted cocoon–

Sloping a handful of change
When I pocketed her, she whispered,
Begging me to spend her
I refused, I refused to even throw her in any bank–
Some poor coffers she'll blend with,
And I'll never again hear her voice.
She clattered every night,
Until i groped her
One foul restless morning, when
With barely a thought in my mind, I spent her.
she laughed, the machine gurgled
And vomited a can of Coca Cola,
So I left it there
Maybe my lover can quench some other's thirst

She's Just Like me

Completely different
Often wrong when she's right
Often desolate and desperate,
Hanging off her worry,
Betrayed by self pity.
She's drowning
A thousand dreams flit
Like loose pages in an ocean
They're wet, ruined, the ink smears
Dreams wilt and memories bleed,
While time seizes our souls.
She's just like me

Angel

The hallow galaxy of swirling fire bellowed apathy
Where silver pinions lanced olive-hued skies,
The seasons snivelled from their communal durance.
The angel descended and it's starving gaze severed forests,
While it meditated above the idiot seas
It's placid passions ululated as it handed forth God's pacts
This angel, who leered with a message and thusly birthed
zealotry from its cold womb,
Relinquished a crown of Heaven's grace.

Kill The Romantic

How wondrous and taciturn—

A soul nestled between the court's marble platforms,
Where I first saw her.
For Her hair was of raven's soul
With a wit that invigorates fire
When hands skimmed across a cheek—
And eagerly over her ascetic eyes.
She ceased dancing while
My image snagged in her mirrors
She was of a sun carrying ephemeral adoration
And It's mismatched hands divided revelries
If she delved into glazed truths trapped in pages,
She wandered abroad, so
I exalted her as the earth ought to,
For she should be revered as a god

We Smoked All Night

A Solemn moon gawked at our cars' hood
Smoke eddied, catching on grime caked to the doors
Heaven was in the flame, it's tobacco grace carried us on—
We Smoked for hours.

When I glimpsed your eyes
They reflected the dissociated boy
Who's wrist you impulsively mimicked

We hooted at our dashboard soundtrack
A small moment when Cash's sorrow
Uplifted the nicotine stained car.

So, like a game, you flicked open another carton,
Gesturing me to slake my agony
Light up, drown in the haze
Die with a stick at your fingers
While ash crowds my lap

We've Lost So Much In Wars and Wrath

Great men die—
Great men will die—
Great men have died ultimately and without reservation
No one will be spared, not one soul
No youth, elder, father, son, rich, or poor
No doctor, scholar, or dreamer
Who thought themselves immortal

For They all died
For Heaven and pride
Casting off self interest to serve a higher cause
Is this what they wanted?

They died miserably or in good health
Surrounded by love, or gunned down in a battlefield,
Hung upon death worn gallows,
But shepherded to paradise on horse-drawn

Every soul we will mark, every life shall be remembered—
Not by their faces, nor by their names
But through a banquet of adoration,
A moment of solidarity that we are not them.
But who have given everything for us
For that they deserve every honour

Heaven Journal

Heaven is a journal
Pens, pencils and markers
scribbled over its pages
We're its' keepsakes—
Little saints—
These reminders tucked
Cozily in paradise

We Sat Dining On Honeydew Melons

And laid in grass beds
Stars mated in space's distant reaches
Where a universe recited a song
That burned away every moon.
We watched clouds melt into the night
And unspoken desire dug its' talons into my neck
While its beak parted, whispering my next line
Where I will be laid to rest
In this coffin of small talk
How cruel—
When my go-to line involves
Pointing out your flaws

I Hated You From The Moment You Appeared

I hated that scarlet dress

I hated how you sat
I hated the words twirling from your crimson lips
And the yellow vowels touching an edge of my arm

I hated you as smoke billowed around us
I hated you as I propped you up against a cedar post
I hated when our lips touched
I hated your breasts pressed against my chest.

The blues scuffed the nights' hollow cheek,
And I hated the night after, we spent right there again
Watching the stars as I curled into your shell
I hate it now more than ever,
Thinking about how we tossed in that bed of play

I hate this longing. I hate you
I hate the thing that took you
And knowing you will never return

The Dance

Amalgam thoughts and streets of ice and iron bars
She danced along boundless nights
Borderless lights cast overhead
I couldn't help but dream a thousand days ahead
Where truth held lockstep with fantasy

A friend of a friend lost in a second
Having feared the negative, I plucked it
But I looked through dimming lights,
The couples knotted together melting into the song
And there you were, yet I hesitated
Not out of fear, why fear that which has no bearing
I hesitated not because I feared rejection— maybe I'm lying

I didn't do it, I wasn't afraid
When I couched fear in a litany, I felt it, drank it,
I was at peace, yet there you were
—Maybe I'm lying
I was afraid you'd say yes
Time is fickle, how it laughs

Jesting sing-song like
And I'd hate to dance with you to a scornful melody,
Its impermanence punctuating ours.
But this is an excuse
A poem to rationalise

An excuse— to write
I repeat it every night since,
Clutching my ignorance
While the dance fades into my memories
To fuel my art further

Stigmata

Vitality drains from my hands
Like poison into the cup,
While I exalt you,
who's crown cleaves my forehead
Yet I sing your wishes
When stained glass sermons glow heavenly

Shreds of the incense clouds whisper an evangelist's plea
And candle wax pitpats into saucers amongst brothers
Kneeling at God's stomach

Their odes require confession in corners
Tucked at Christ's breast.
Their hymns demand our vows,
Our promised hearts offered up for its fears to languish

My side howls from Longinus' wrath
Exposing a wound that seeps my passions on its scarlet lips
This is a gift— divinity made flesh;
Our Lord's torment embraces me

And I accept it modestly,
Brimming with gratitude for God's Grace
Ineffable as it is and all loving
Amen.

Celestial Birds

Birds vexed the eyes that watched the—
And observed a set of—
Aware of things jostling about

Brown lumps squished beneath little shoes
Ambling into the grass to play,
Where she watched an opulent flock perch on branches

While they observed her— curiously
Her youthful desolation guttered
Her brain droned, trying to sort its' faculties

The floor is an unseen plane while she trods across it
Yet, the mess of birds pounced, enclosing her in its ephemeral din
Who's hum settled awareness into her mind,
Sorting it's capacities and putting her in order
Before vanishing

She sat there looking around the kitchen
The floor is a floor— wooden planks
Glued beneath countertops

A stove which burns when touched
Feet to walk, hands to grab
Joys unmistakably giggled for two parents
Who smile at their joyous child
Engaged to reality

The Poet and The Soldier

A Poet once fell in love with a soldier

He wrote a thousand poems to honour her long stay at war
He wrote of Christmas and Easter eves
Spent, while the soldier fought at distant plains.

He taped verse to a hearth
A last ode declaring every love
Once stuffed in his heart's compartments.
He revered his pen, cuddling it like a lover—
A surrogate till his soldier returned

She, however, brandished her bayonet
and it dragged on the sky
The clouds ripped, pouring rain,
so she sat there at his doorstep
Watching the cuts she had weaved.

Little intricate verses forming a poem
A simple promise, for when the poet checked his steps
The two sat there swapping love and declared
No more separation.

Evelyn McHale

Did you think You'd be remembered like this?
Life's epoch frozen at the end
A misery crashed.
They rushed your body off, but you knew
There wasn't much anyone could save
So they proclaimed you dead at the scene.
They found the note where you leapt
You figured your tendencies deserved an unceremonious end
You were no distinction and requested no ceremony,
No site to mend your grief
But you failed to see what you'd become —
The most beautiful suicide

About The Author:

Blace Alcock is an upstart poet and author with dreams of having enough money to buy food; nothing fancy, bread and olive oil would suffice. He is currently engaged in an active war against the dreaded poetic curse of too many words, so he'll cut this short. He's Canadian and talks like it too. His igloo is always cozy and his typewriter welcoming. When he isn't writing, he's reading... about writing, and you can find him on Instagram at @bwoyken438. He does things there, but you'll have to find that out for yourself.

www.ingramcontent.com/pod-product-compliance
Lightning Source LLC
Chambersburg PA
CBHW060509160726
47992CB00003B/1400